Shirley W Hall

The Law of Impersonation as Applied to Abstract Ideas and

Religious Dogmas

Shirley W Hall

The Law of Impersonation as Applied to Abstract Ideas and Religious Dogmas

ISBN/EAN: 9783744678551

Printed in Europe, USA, Canada, Australia, Japan

Cover: Foto ©Lupo / pixelio.de

More available books at **www.hansebooks.com**

THE LAW

OF

IMPERSONATION.

THE LAW

OF

IMPERSONATION

AS APPLIED TO

ABSTRACT IDEAS AND RELIGIOUS DOGMAS.

BY

S. W. HALL.

" Now comes the pain of Truth, to whom 'tis pain;
O folly! for to bear all naked truths,
And to envisage circumstance, all calm,
That is the top of sovereignty."

Hyperion.

LONDON:

GEORGE MANWARING (Successor of John Chapman),
8, KING WILLIAM STREET, STRAND.
MDCCCLXI.

LONDON:

STRANGEWAYS & WALDEN (late G. BARCLAY), Printers,
28 Castle St. Leicester Sq.

PREFACE.

AMONGST the signs of the times which have prompted the publication of the present Book is the favourable reception by the Public of the now celebrated "Essays and Reviews." All honour to the courageous initiative of the learned Professors and Divines of Oxford and Cambridge in their efforts to eliminate the Supernatural out of Christianity, and to establish its fundamental doctrines on the basis of Faith and Truth, and not on the traditions and dogmas of by-gone ages.

This move at Oxford had already been preceded by the Development Theory of Dr. Newman, qualified too much, however, by the unnecessary intervention of intermittent special Revelation.

The Puseyite or Tractarian tendencies are another sign of the times, showing that the religious convictions of society are becoming uneasy and unsettled; and, on the other hand, the Parliamentary majorities in favour of the Abolition of Church-rates indicate the spread of Nonconformist individual opinions, and, consequently, dissatisfaction with the Articles and Creeds of our Established Church.

It is time the Church of England laid out her foundations anew on a larger scale and broader basis so as to be truly the mother of all, and a National Church with good will and welcome to all reasonable Christians; and why not an Imperial Church, expanding her religious sympathies, and making her sphere of action, commensurate with the extent of the British empire and the political domination of the British races?

We are probably on the eve of great religious changes and events. If the Papacy, clearing itself of obsolete dogmas, revert to the purer principles of Christianity in alliance with the liberties of Italy, there will ensue the birth of new opinions and new tendencies more in harmony with the intellectual position of the century. The Italians, with their genius for synthetical generalization, will then again take the lead of the world in religious thought and action, and go beyond the positive Protestantism of the North.

CONTENTS.

viii CONTENTS.

CONTENTS.

CONTENTS.

THE

LAW OF IMPERSONATION.

I.

THE LAW OF IMPERSONATION AS APPLIED TO THE DEVELOPMENT
OF CHRISTIANITY.

THE time has now come when we can consider
Christianity as the result of the progressive development of our Psychical and religious nature, from
the first creation of man to our present times,
and when we can anticipate its further progress,
in the future, out of the Symbolism and Impersonation in which its doctrines have hitherto been
invested, to its final triumph in Spirit and in Truth
amongst all the nations of the earth.   From the
infant periods of the world down to those in which
we now live, mankind have viewed religious truths
through the medium of the Perceptive part of the

B

mind, acting in alliance with Faith and Mysticism, and the result has necessarily been to invest them with a form of Impersonation. Abstract ideas and spiritual sentiments have been impersonated and made divine, and then considered as Objective realities, which is, in great part, the present condition of Christianity, just as the Impersonations of nature and of the internal consciousness were indivinized and worshipped in the times of Pagan antiquity.

When these Impersonations are viewed and analysed by the higher intellectual element of Reason, they are found to be nothing more than the physical and moral laws of the world. Psychical and religious ideas are then apprehended in the Abstract, whereas Perception by itself views them under the Concrete forms of Symbol and Impersonation.

Thus the agencies of nature, the motive passions and pursuits of man, were personified by the undeveloped mind of the antients, and formed the divinities of their mythologies. When these lost their hold and disappeared with the progress of thought, and the appointed development of Humanity, a new series of Impersonations of a higher class succeeded, viz. the Impersonations of the religious truths and ideas of Christianity. The spiritual forms of being within the soul of man were transfigured objectively by the action of the Perceptive mind. The Psychical convictions, which make up Faith, underwent the process of Impersonation, and hence arose the transcendental mythology of Christianity from the same mental necessity and by the same process as the Pagan mythologies of the East, Egypt, Greece, Rome, Scandinavia, and other regions of the world.

A general apprehension of the laws of Nature and Mind replaced the Pagan Impersonations of antiquity. Reason viewed them under the Abstract form of causality, and they disappeared after fulfilling their provisional mission in the progress of Humanity. The Christian Impersonations are fated to undergo the same process as the Pagan. When apprehended in their internal significance by the reflective mind; when elevated to the height of Abstract Ideas, the transitive form of the Concrete —the Impersonated—will have seen its day, and Christianity will have been evolved in Spirit and in Truth. Its furthest possible development will then have been accomplished, and mankind will have entered the last and highest stage of religious and Psychical progress—the union of Faith and Reason. Then will have been fulfilled the prophetic covenant of old, and the supreme law of God's Providence—the Unity and Brotherhood of the World.

II.

THE LAW OF IMPERSONATION AS APPLIED TO THE PAGAN MYTHOLOGIES.

In primitive times, when men observed the forces and phenomena of Nature, they were impressed with an idea of power, by their order, design, and regularity, and they attributed the exercise of this power to the intelligent personality of some Divine being: Hence there was Jupiter for the heavens, Neptune for the sea, Apollo for the sun, Pan for universal nature, and Fauns, Nymphs, Dryads, Oreads, Nereids, &c., for the woods, the mountains, and the waves. The same process of Impersonation was applied to the moral forces and phenomena of their internal consciousness — to their sentiments and passions: hence Minerva, Venus Aphrodite, Eros and Anteros, for wisdom, beauty, and love; hence Psychè, the Graces, and the coarser divinities of the Eleusinian and Phallic mysteries. Impressed with deep feelings of providential agency (*Prisca fides*), they applied also the same process of mind to the events and pursuits of life: Ceres, Mercury, Diana, and Mars, were the divinities presiding over agriculture, commerce, hunting, and war; and fate and fortune were personified in Bonus Eventus, Fortuna, Nemesis, the Parcæ, and the Sibyls. Again, their δαίμων was an objective form of the individual consciousness. A like process of Impersonation was applied to their rudiments of Faith in another life, and the action of Conscience upon the crimes and misdeeds of men; as in the Dii Inferi, Pluto, Minos and Rhadamanthus, and the Furies.

Unable at that early period of civilization to apprehend generally the relation of cause and effect in the laws of Nature, they found a solution of the idea in supposed personal agency acting in a mysterious manner upon the world and Humanity at large, and the subjective phenomena of their own minds. And this personal interposition was more especially recognised in political crises of great danger, or on occasion of events of portentous meaning—eclipses, auroras, comets, thunderbolts, and earthquakes—when auguries and religious ceremonies were solemnly performed to deprecate the anger or hostile intentions of the supposed preternatural agency of the Impersonations of their own minds—the gods and divinities of their mythologies.

This arose from the impossibility of their apprehending Abstract ideas as embodied in the laws of Nature. The ancients were constrained by the undeveloped state of their intellectual system to adopt the notion of personal agency—

to see Causation in the Concrete—and thence to impersonate and indivinize the physical and moral forces of the world.   And as the same process obtained in all the nations of antiquity, it may therefore be regarded as a Law of Impersonation of Abstract Ideas, because their reason being both undeveloped and untrained, they employed only the activity of Perception to interpret the phenomena and their causation—a metaphysical instrument unequal to the task.   Hence the origin of their Impersonations—visible forms resulting from, and addressed to, the perceptive faculties of the mind, which, at that early stage of civilization, were in vigorous and characteristic activity.

This law supplies an explanation of the mythological Impersonations of all the infant periods of the world in barbarous nations as well as in the more elaborate religious systems of Egypt and the East.   It explains also the universal Impersonation of ideas and moral qualities (Justice, Charity, Hope, Time, Death, &c.); and it shows how even the characteristics of the earlier heroic ages were mythically individualized and embodied in one ideal personage, as in Hercules, for heroic exploits, feats of strength, and personal prowess ; in Hermes, for discoveries in the arts; in Homer, for poetic legends; in Solon, for the principles of law and jurisprudence, &c.

By the natural progress of society, and the dissemination of philosophic ideas, the Impersonations of classical antiquity lost all authority over the minds of men. They were dethroned and supplanted by the higher mystic Impersonations of Christianity, which still prevail, to be superseded in their turn hereafter by the spiritual truths themselves.

" The intelligible forms of ancient poets,
" The fair humanities of old religion,
" The Power, the Beauty, and the Majesty,
" That had her haunts in dale or piny mountain,
" Or forest, by slow stream, or pebbly spring,
" Or chasms and wat'ry depths ; all these 've vanished.
" They live no longer in the Faith of Reason."

COLERIDGE.

III.

NECESSITY OF IMPERSONATION IN TEACHING RECONDITE PSYCHICAL TRUTHS.

The Bible is one continuous example of the law of Impersonation from the personal Fiats of Genesis to the Esoteric teaching of Christ and St. Paul.

This mode of exhibiting recondite psychical truths to the mass of mankind is a matter of necessity. Their unaccomplished mental development absolutely requires Abstract Ideas to be

presented under sensible images, and causation
to be interpreted by personal agency. (Moses,
Mahomet, Numa Pompilius, Catholic Legends.)
This difficulty of expounding spiritual ideas, and
the divine authority of Truth and Conscience, was
ever present in the mind of Christ (Nicodemus,
Woman of Samaria). In order to bring home to
rude understandings the force of moral laws, He
was obliged to couch his precepts and doctrines
in the language of one having a direct personal
mission from God himself. Nothing less than a
sensible corporeal medium with articulate organs,
could evoke their latent Faith, or satisfy their
belief. With this aid alone were they able to
realize the idea of God, His laws of Conscience,
and a Future state of Being. For their easier
comprehension the Spiritual and the Intellectual
were brought down to Sense. Hence the present
necessity for Esoteric interpretation, to restore the
ideas and doctrine of Christ, and St. Paul, to their
essential abstract form. " The hour cometh and
" now is when the true worshippers shall worship
" the Father in Spirit and in Truth."—"Because
" seeing they see not, and hearing they hear not,
" neither do they understand."—"I will open my
" mouth in parables; I will utter things that have
" been kept secret from the foundation of the
" world."—"The natural man receiveth not the

" things of the Spirit of God ; for they are fool-
" ishness unto him : neither can he know them,
" because they are spiritually discerned."—" The
" Light shineth in darkness; and the darkness
" comprehended it not."—"When for the time ye
" ought to be teachers, ye have need that one
" teach you again which be the first principles
" of the oracles of God; and are become such
" as have need of milk, and not of strong meat.
" For every one that useth milk is unskilful in
" word of righteousness : for he is a babe. But
" strong meat belongeth to them that are of full
" age, even those who by reason of use have their
" senses exercised to discern both good and evil."

IV.

OBJECTIVE PERCEPTION VIEWS ABSTRACT IDEAS UNDER A FORM
OF IMPERSONATION.

There are three things we cannot compass—
Matter, First Causation, and God.

We cannot understand the creation of some-
thing out of nothing, or the annihilation of Matter.

The existence of Matter is for us an ultimate
fact. It exists because it exists.

First Causation is an ultimate idea. It is the
limit of our intellectual system.

We know the existence of Matter by Perception, and not by Reason. It cannot, therefore, be proved by any process of ratiocination.

We apprehend First Causation by Reason, and not by Perception.

The pure Deist apprehends God through the idea of First Causation, objectively.

The pure Pietist knows God through Faith, or Psychical conviction, subjectively.

The Christian Philosopher knows God through Faith and First Causation, both subjectively and objectively.

Thus there are two modes of knowing God, viz. by Reason and by Faith; one intellectual, and the other psychical, both being, however, equally constituent parts of our nature.

If we attempt to apprehend God through Faith and Perception alone, Impersonation results from that mode of apprehending the Divinity. Hence Fetichism, Idolatry, Animal worship, and the Mythologies. Hence the Mystic Person of Christ, and the Three Persons of the Trinity.

The innate subjective psychical idea of God exists, in more or less force, in all the races of man.

Hence the knowledge of God through Faith.

Where their intellectual system is weak and

incompletely developed, the form of Impersonation corresponds to the deficiency, as in savage tribes, and the earlier nations of antiquity.

Where intellectual progress has been made, the Impersonated form becomes grander and more elevated, as in the cultivated classes of European society.

But as soon as men become capable of apprehending the abstract idea of God through First Causation, and they conjoin it with the psychical conviction of God through Faith, all Impersonations vanish, and the last step in the philosophical and religious knowledge of the Divinity has been attained.

V.

THE ATONING CONSCIENCE OF THE SOUL IMPERSONATED IN CHRIST.

But besides the twofold idea of God, there exists in man an innate profound Faith in the eternal Truth and Justice of the Divine Power. This Faith resides in the organic constitution of our psychical Conscience. It is a constituent part of our higher nature, perceiving, with the light of reason, Good and Evil, Right and Wrong, Truth and Error; one of its supreme functions being to reconcile our individual acts and thoughts with this idea of God's justice by means of the re-generating process of spiritual Self-Atonement — the sublime discovery and doctrine of Christ, with which his name is for ever identified, and of which his death and Passion are the external symbols.

The first rudiments of the Atoning Conscience can be traced in the Jewish ceremonial, and still more so, in the precepts and practice of Pythagoras.

This atoning Conscience in the soul, and the Love of Humanity, are identical with the Christ within us—" the true Light which lighteth every " man that cometh into the world." It has been most truly and most worthily impersonated in the Mystic Person of Christ—an objective form of the inner spiritual equivalent, but which could only be thus well and practically apprehended by the mass of mankind,—unable to realize the Abstract moral idea unless projected externally under a Concrete form, owing to their incomplete intellectual de-velopment. Like the foregoing impersonation of the Deity by Faith and Perception alone, the same combination has here again impersonated the Atoning Conscience. The time will come when Faith and Reason together will supersede this provisional form of Truth.

VI.

THE INTELLIGIBLE INTERPRETED AS THE SUPERNATURAL, WITHOUT THE LIGHT OF REASON.

But besides the Known World, there exists the Unknown World—the Infinite Unknown.

The limits of the Known World are the finite limits of the Human Mind.

There is therefore Another World, transcending our finite nature, infinite as God, Matter, Space, Numbers, and Eternity.

Independently of its demonstration by reason, God has implanted in man—deposited in his soul, a mystic Sense, Desire and Hope of this other Unknown World, rudimentally expressed in all the religious Creeds and Sepulchral Monuments of antiquity, and in the theological dogma of the Resurrection of the Body.

This Mystic Sense, unenlightened by knowledge, brings improperly the Supernatural within the legitimate domain of the Intellectual, and acting in conjunction with Perception alone, and without Reason, again impersonates, as in the cases already mentioned, the spiritual ideas and activities of the Soul, impersonates the Divine Light within us, so that the heavenly spaces become peopled by ideal hosts and hierarchies of

Angels and Archangels and the Mystic Persons of the Trinity.   The Third Person of the Trinity, as representing the *Numen*, or active form of God within us, likewise displays its presence objectively under the Symbol of the Dove or of Cloven Tongues of Fire.

By this Mystic Sense of the Supernatural, acting without the aid and warrant of intellectual enquiry, the Intelligible and the Known become regarded as the Unknown.   Hence Superstition in science and religion — alchemy and mesmerism on the one hand, and theological dogmas and fables on the other.   The providential agency of God is viewed under the grosser forms of miraculous interpositions and external revelation, and His wondrous ways are brought down to the lower standards of Sense and Perception.

VII.

FAITH THE EXPRESSION OF INNATE PSYCHICAL POWER.

Faith then proceeds from three spiritual elements in our Psychical nature; viz.

1. Our innate subjective sense of God and Providential agency in, and around, us.
2. Our Atoning Conscience and sense of Truth and Justice.

3. Our innate subjective belief in the Immortality of the Soul, and the existence of Another Unknown World.

The subjective activity of these Psychical principles in conjunction with Reason, constitutes the highest form of true Faith, being "the substance " of things hoped for, the evidence of things not " seen," as written by God himself in the tablets of the human Soul: "I will put my laws into " their hearts and in their minds will I write " them." This development of spiritual ideas, from Symbol and Impersonation, to Truth itself is the consummation of the Second Advent of Christ upon earth " in Spirit and in Truth."

VIII.

DISTINCTION BETWEEN FAITH AND DOGMA.

It is necessary to distinguish between Faith and Dogma.

Faith is the voice of God within the Soul. It is the expression of the various psychical powers He has deposited within our nature, to tell us of His existence and Providential agency, of His presence within the soul, to warn us from sin by the light of our Judging and Atoning Conscience, and to guide and cheer us with the hope of fulfilling the purpose of our being in a Future World —

germs of Truth and Grace sown broadcast throughout the various nations of the earth, under different forms, and in different degrees, according to the type of race, but universal in their diffusion, and obeying the same law of development, progress, and of destiny—" That was the true Light which " lighteth every man that cometh into the world."

Dogma, on the contrary, is the work and language of man in his struggle to arrive at Divine Truth. It is a transitory form of belief subject to error and to being wrongly interpreted. It is an essential constituent of all the theologies of the world—those of Brahmah, of Buddha, of the Asiatic systems, of Egypt, Greece, and Rome, and, lastly, of the different denominations of the Christian Church ; the difference of their dogmas being the chief badge of distinction between them. It is therefore not Divine Faith, but human Dogma, to believe in Transubstantiation, Purgatory, the Incarnation of God, the Trinity, the Divine Right of Kings, Inspiration, the Infallibility of the Pope and the Bible, Miracles, Prophecies, and external Revelations, the Fall of Man, Original Sin, the Vicarious Atonement, the Resurrection of the Body, and the Day of Judgment. These dogmas represent, more or less, recondite truths of the deepest import to mankind. The dogmas will one day perish under philosophic inquiry, with the systems of which they form part, but the Truth which is in them will survive, for, like Faith, it is immortal, and ever coming from God and the depths of nature to illuminate the heart and reason of man.

IX.

THE THEOLOGICAL DIVINITY OF CHRIST ANALYSED.

The theological Dogma of the Divinity of Christ will be found to consist of the following elements, as analysed by the Law of Impersonation, viz.

1. The living historic person of Christ.
2. The Impersonation of his characteristic nature, and Principles of Doctrine, viz. The Love of Humanity, and the Conscience Judging and Atoning in the sight of God.
3. The fusion of these two elements, by the theological process of Incarnation, into one idea, viz. the Divinity of Christ, the Second Person of the Trinity.

X.

THE INCARNATION OF CHRIST A CONSEQUENCE OF HIS THEOLOGICAL IMPERSONATION.

The Divine Light within us having been thus impersonated, made God, and conjoined with the

c

living person of Christ by the early Christians, the doctrine of the Incarnation would follow as a logical consequence. It would form the connecting link between two distinct things—the Human Person, and the principle Impersonated and Indivinized; between the Abstract Idea and its Concrete expression. It would be a consummation of the union of the Spiritual with the Real in one Person—the theologically-made Christ, as God and Man—the Second Person of the Trinity.

XI.

A MYSTIC LOCALITY NECESSARY FOR IMPERSONATED IDEAS.

The spiritual activities of our nature being thus embodied, and made divine, under concrete visible forms, by the Law of Impersonation, it necessarily follows, that these objective creations must inhabit some place of abode. Thus the mystic locality of the classical divinities of antiquity was in the ranges of Mount Olympus, that of the Scandinavian races in the Valhalla, that of the Hindoos in the Himalayas, that of the Mahometans midway between the earth and heavens; whilst that of the Christian Impersonations is in Heaven, peopled by departed saints, the angelic hosts, the Virgin Mother of Christ, and the mystic Persons of the Trinity. So again, our Faith in the Immortality of the Soul

is objectively transfigured by the visible resurrection and ascension of our bodies; and the
subjective activity of our psychical Conscience, and
guilty Fears, finds an equivalent collective expression in the awful dramatic imagery of the Last
Judgment, the Fires of Hell, and the grim Impersonations of the Devil and Death.

Let us be thankful, that Hell, Acheron, and
Fear, are conquered by Faith, and knowledge of
First Causation.

XII.

THE NECESSITY OF THE IDEA OF VICARIOUS ATONEMENT, FROM OUR CONSCIENCE BEING LATE IN ORDER OF DEVELOPMENT.

The idea of Vicarious Atonement was evidently
forced upon the first Christians by necessity—
by the conscious inability of the individual
to satisfy of himself the Truth and Justice of
God. Such a power was not in him. It is the
proper function of the Moral Sense to atone for sin
and error by repentance and reformation, and so
reconcile the conscience with God, but the great
mass of mankind is now, and ever has been, most
deficient in this particular duty; hence the necessity for touching and affecting their rudimental conscience by an external image of sacrifice, addressed
to the Perception of sense, and suited to their

ideas of Divine Justice; and what image could be presented more overwhelming to the imagination and human sympathy, than the incidents and significance of the Passion of Christ, whose personality in their eyes comprehended both God and Man, and whose death supplied a collective idea of Atonement, commensurate with the vast sum of the sins of imperfect Humanity. No better scheme for developing and educating the first growth of the human conscience could possibly have been desired, and it will certainly prevail, until the Moral Sense emerges out of its present rudimental stage, and Christ, as the Spirit of Truth, comes a second time on earth into the minds and hearts of men.

XIII.

THE TRINITY, THEOLOGICAL IMPERSONATIONS OF PSYCHICAL IDEAS.

The origin of the Trinity must be sought in the Impersonations of the Spiritual Entities, or Activities, composing the Human Soul. Thus,

1. Our subjective Psychical idea of God, impersonated by Objective Perception, is represented as the First Person of the Trinity, as God the Father, the Creator.
2. By the same process, the Divine element

in Man, impersonated as God by the Brahmins, and biblically characterized as the Christ in us, the Light of the World, the Word, the λογος, — synonyms of the Judging and Atoning Conscience of the Soul in the presence of God — has been impersonated, and made God, in the Person of Christ, as the Second Person of the Trinity, the Son of God, the Saviour and Redeemer.

3. By the same process of Objective Perception, our Mystic sense of Divine agency in the Soul has been impersonated, as the Third Person of the Trinity, the Holy Ghost, the Paraclete, the Comforter, the Spirit of Truth.

Hence the theological idea and expression of the Three Persons of the Trinity remount to the same source, viz. the spiritual entities existing in the Psychical constitution of man having been impersonated and translated from Subjective to Objective forms of Being; so that it may be truly said, they acknowledge the same Hypostasis, or Substance, belong to one and the same system, and equally participate in the same transcendental origin. In other words, they are the Trinity in Unity, and Unity in Trinity, consubstantial and co-equal.

XIV.

THE TRINITY WILL MERGE INTO UNITY WHEN DIVESTED OF ITS FORM OF IMPERSONATION.

But just as the multiform Divinities of the Old World became merged in the idea of the Unity of God, so the Three Mystic modes of the Being of God in the Trinity, as Creator, Redeemer, and Comforter, will, with a larger application of intellectual power, merge in the idea of One God, operating by Law and Means to an End, within the spiritual interior of Humanity, as demonstrated by Reason and confirmed by Faith.

XV.

CHRISTIAN IMPERSONATIONS PROVISIONAL ONLY.

The Indivinization of Christ gradually obtained as the old Pagan Impersonations died away. It was already a popular belief when the Bishops of the Nicene Council established it as a Theological Dogma. But, as said before, the Christian Impersonations will sooner or later decline, like the Pagan, as Reason becomes conjoined with Faith, engendering Abstract spiritual ideas. It is then we shall see and worship God in Spirit and in Truth.

" When that which is perfect is come, then that
" which is in part shall be done away.

" When I was a child, I spake as a child, I
" understood as a child, l thought as a child : but
" when I became a man, I put away childish things.
" For now we see through a glass, darkly; but
" then face to face : now I know in part; but then
" shall I know even also as I am known."

XVI.

KNOWLEDGE OF GOD BY REASON AND BY FAITH.

There are two ways of arriving at a knowledge
of God, one Intellectual, the other Psychical.

The *first* is by Causality and Induction, as
evidenced in the works of the philosophic Deists,
of whom Hume is an excellent example, and in
those of Cudworth, Butler, Paley, and the Bridge-
water writers on Natural Theology.

The *second* is by Faith, or the innate Psychical
intuition of God, independent of Reason, or intellectual perception. It is the spiritual or subjective
perception of God, as dwelling in our Soul, and
forms an integral part of the Psychical system of
man. This spiritual knowledge of God constitutes
the chief basis of Christianity. It was partially
seen by Pythagoras and Plato. It inspired the

Jewish Patriarchs and Prophets, and became impersonated, as Jehovah, in the religious Faith of the Jews. It burned intensely in the souls of the first Christians, and the Roman Catholic Pietists of later times, St. Francis and St. Theresa. It illustrated by its influence the Umbrian School of Painters, Fra Angelico, Perugino, and the divine Raphael; and it is constantly displaying itself with unabated fervour in the works of love, piety, and deep religious faith of modern times.

Mere rudiments of its presence exist in Fetichism, and Deistic Impersonation, amongst infant nations, and the inferior races of man.

Both these modes (the Intellectual and Psychical) make the knowledge of God irresistible. It is the union of Philosophy and Religion. It is seeing God in Spirit and in Truth.

XVII.

THE ABSTRACT AND CONCRETE IDEAS OF GOD.

The Impersonation of God is the idea of God in the Concrete, the Abstract idea being apprehended by Reason, the Concrete by Objective Perception. The latter mode is more agreeable to the mass of mankind; the former, to the philosophic mind.

So the Resurrection of the Body is the Concrete Perception of our Psychical intuition of Another Life. The idea could not be realised by the Many unless invested with this material form. It would have no existence for them. Hence the absolute necessity for such a mode of teaching. It is the first step in Faith.

XVIII.

OUR IDEA OF GOD CORRESPONDS TO THE PERFECTION OF OUR MIND AND SOUL.

When Faith and Objective Perception work together, there is a mental necessity to impersonate the Being of God. But when Faith and Reflective Reason act together, then God is seen in Spirit and in Truth. Our conception of the Deity expands and enlarges according to the perfection of our Mind and Soul; and it is therefore small and contracted amongst the uneducated classes of society, and in the infant ages of the world.

XIX.

THE IMPERSONATIONS OF OUR IDEAS ASSUME DRAMATIC ACTION.

Having thus given personal forms to our spiritual idea of God (the Father), to the Atoning

Conscience of the Soul (Christ), and to our Subjective sense of Divine Agency (the Holy Ghost),
and having impersonated as Angels the general
activities of our Psychical powers, whilst in communion with God ; the Laws of mind required, that
these Objective images should be projected in space,
and located somewhere in relation to each other.
Hence, as said before, arose the idea of Heaven
and Paradise, as the fit habitation of the spiritual
embodiments of the Christian mythology, as Olympus was the abode of the Pagan divinities preceding
them.   Hence the idea of Hell, as the fit abode of
Satan and his fallen angels — the corresponding
Impersonations of Sin, Wickedness, and Crime.

These various Impersonations of the active
forces of the Soul, and of Human Nature, being
thus brought into one ideal locality, and into one
system, could not fail to assume dramatic action,
each playing a part according to its special quality
of Being, and its logical relation to the chief subject of the drama—that wonderful being Man—
with all his mystic traditions of the Past, and all
his hopes of the Future.   Thus the Law of the
Atonement—the key-stone of our human system—
was presented to the understanding, as God sending his Beloved Son to save the world; our Faith
in Truth and Divine Agency, as the sending and
descent of the Holy Ghost.   The Divine authority

of Truth, as exercised by Christ, was symbolized as
" the Spirit descending from heaven like a Dove,"
or as seeing "Heaven open, and angels of God
ascending and descending upon the Son of Man."
The tribunal of our Conscience was collectively
transfigured as the Judgment-seat of Christ, and
the laws of nature and of Humanity were represented everywhere by the personal presence and
fiats of the Almighty and as His special commands.

XX.

THE OBJECTIVE FORMS OF IDEAS HAVE A STRONGER HOLD UPON THE POPULAR MIND THAN THE IDEAS THEMSELVES.

The fondness and partiality of society and unenlightened populations for this species of Objective
representation is evidenced by the Miracle Plays of
former times, by the annual modern dramatic
spectacles of the Nativity, and the Crucifixion,
in the Churches of Rome, and by the popular
rehearsal of the Miracle of St. Januarius in the
Cathedral of Naples. Nothing short of ocular
inspection can bring conviction to rude minds of
the reality of Providential Agency. Indeed the
creative power of our objective imagination cannot
transcend the terrible imagery of the Resurrection
of the Dead, and the Last Judgment; and no
wonder it reigns supreme in the fears, consciences

and minds of man.   The pure spiritual idea of the
Soul's Immortality and a Life to come, might
suffice well enough for Esoteric thinkers, but
would afford very little purchase or hold on the
Faith of the vast majority, who still live in the
stage of Symbol and Impersonation.

XXI.

THE THEOLOGICAL DIVINITY OF CHRIST ESTABLISHED AS A DOGMA BY THE COUNCIL OF NICE.

It was in the Council of Nice, A.D. 325, that
the idea of the twofold nature of Christ was established as an Article of Orthodox faith.   After long
protracted controversies with the Arians, each
party triumphant and defeated in its turn, the more
absolute and mystic dogmas of the Athanasian
Creed were then adopted by the Bishops and
Patriarchs of the Church, as a true exposition of
Christian doctrine, and, as such, they are still to be
found in the Book of Common Prayer.   It is a
curious fact, that no more advanced interpretation
has been made from that time to the present day
—full 1500 years of sealed-up belief—unless the
recent promulgation of the dogma of the Imma-
culate Conception can be called progress, in which
the Virgin Mother of Christ is likewise made the

mother of the Impersonation of a spiritual element
of the soul, so that the combination of twofold
maternity is required to engender his twofold com-
pounded theological nature— a piece of transcendental physiology more in accordance with the superstition of mythic ages than with the philosophic
criterion of the 19th century.

When the first Christians thus attributed the
double character of God and Man to Christ, it was,
as said before, by impersonating the divine portion
of human nature, with which he was so exception-
ally endowed, by the same law and process of
Objective Perception as that, by which the forces
of external nature were impersonated and deified
by their Pagan contemporaries. They conjoined
in one idea our subjective sense of God, and the
great characteristic and discovery of Christ—the
Law of Atonement, as the spiritual function of our
Conscience. It was the Impersonation of this idea
which they indivinized, and then attaching it to
the historic person of Christ, his Godhead became
thus established as the leading Dogma of the
Church. Some generations will probably yet elapse
before the immortal doctrine of the Atonement
will be divested of this theological form, and be
brought back to its spiritual significance as taught
by Christ himself.

XXII.

THE ATONEMENT NOT KNOWN TO THE PHILOSOPHERS AND RELIGIONS OF ANTIQUITY.

The action of a Judging and Atoning Conscience was never embodied as a doctrine in any of the ancient religious systems, or by any of the ancient philosophers, with the very remarkable exception of Pythagoras, the great Sage and Reformer of Magna Grecia, who, like Christ in after ages, appealed to the Moral Conscience and self-abnegation of his disciples with such astounding success, and whose Precepts and Golden Verses still shine upon us, as an illuminated track in the darkness of antiquity. The great defect of the Platonic system was the want of this Supreme law of our spiritual being; so that when the full discovery was announced in all the godlike simplicity of Christ's teaching, it struck a deep responsive chord in the universal human heart, and ever prevailing with the irresistible force of Truth and God's law of Humanity, vanquished all the philosophic and religious systems of the Old World, superseding the lofty moral pride of the Stoics, and perfecting the noble intellectual conceptions of the Platonists.

XXIII.

THE IDEAS OF PLATO AN ESSENTIAL INTELLECTUAL COMPLEMENT OF CHRISTIANITY.

Their great Master, Plato, full of Faith and mystic ideality, was the first to develope formally the doctrine of the Spirituality of the Soul, and its immortal destiny. Ever seeing God's image in the beauty of the visible world, his high-toned expositions of divine truths will one day become an essential intellectual complement of Christian Faith and Philosophy; and it may be truly said, the spirit of the Platonic doctrines will never die as long as the intuitive aspirations of Hope and enlightened Faith make for us a stepping-stone from mortality to the perfection, which is nearer to God. A period seems to be fast approaching in Europe favourable to the revival of the purer part of the Platonic philosophy. There is a prophetic saying of Proclus in his commentaries on the Parmenides, which is curious from the antiquity of the date, and the faith expressed in the future prevalence of the ideas of his Master : " I should say," writes Proclus, " the Platonic form of philosophy " came to the world for the benefit of human " souls; that its principles might survive to a " distant futurity, and that it might be to man in

" the place of statues, of temples and sacred in-
" stitutions, and that it might lead to the salvation
" of the men that now are, and to those who shall
" exist hereafter." And, indeed, the Phædo still
exists to delight and enchant the human mind and
heart; but the symbolic and material monuments
of the different religions of antiquity—the fanes,
the temples and hierarchies of Egypt, Greece and
Rome, and even of less ancient times, have passed,
or are now passing away, in proportion as advance-
ment in abstract and generalised ideas impels the
intellectual classes of society to leave aside the
provisional Impersonations of their Objective Perception.

XXIV.

NECESSITY OF ESOTERIC TEACHING BY THE ANCIENT PHILOSOPHERS AND BY CHRIST.

In the ancient religious and philosophic systems
(of Egypt, Greece, Rome, the Jews, the Brahmins,
&c.) the more recondite moral truths were represented to the Vulgar under outward symbolic forms,
whilst the more advanced disciples were initiated in
their inner intellectual, or Esoteric meaning. And
this arose from the proven impossibility of the
human mind, when not intellectually developed,
understanding the force of Abstract truths, and

Abstract ideas. Thus the abstract idea of First Causation, and of God, was rudimentally represented by the collective individual divinities of the old Pagan mythologies, just as the Psychical idea of the Atonement is expressed by all denominations of Christians in the present day by the Concrete image of Christ crucified, and his Vicarious sacrifice for the sins of the world. This mode of presenting Truth through a glass, darkly, could not have been otherwise, in order to reach understandings moulded in the forms of past ideas and past traditions. It was necessary, too, in self-defence against the misapprehension of ignorance, and the natural resentment of religious prejudice. Thus at Athens, when Anaxagoras first taught the unity of the Supreme Being and of the Universe, it required all the influence of Pericles to save him from public prosecution, and the fatal hemlock on a charge of atheism and impiety, just as, a few generations back, the Christian authorities of Europe put to death without mercy, and with unrelenting severity, pious divines, philosophers, original thinkers, men of genius, and whole populations, for calling in question, or differently interpreting, the dogmas, doctrines, moral idols, and miraculous pretensions of the so-called Orthodox Churches. At Athens, again, the fate of Socrates teaches us how necessary

D

it is to veil our true and more advanced intellectual
opinions in Esoteric secresy,—how necessary to
employ like him the popular form of symbolic
language in order to be understood by the gene-
rality of men. To save ourselves from the usual
charge of impiety and atheism, we must, like him,
make appearance, and sacrifice our cock to Æscu-
lapius, the only language intelligible to the vulgar.

The rulers and legislators of infant nations have
ever been recorded to materialize, so to speak, the
more elevated ranges of thought to the level of the
unaccomplished mental development of the great
mass, whose very nature it is to regard principles
and intellectual abstractions through an embodied
individualization, and to require absolutely some
outward and visible sign to meet their limited power
of apprehension, so that to their minds the higher
kinds of knowledge are, of necessity, incompre-
hensible. These are to them the unknown tongues
of St. Paul, requiring interpretation, and they may
be said to stand only in the outward vestibule of
the spiritual world, where they gaze with the
wonder of ignorance on the differently pictured
forms of the veil which divides them from the
sacred tabernacle containing the first mystic truths
of the Universe. And it was a favourite saying of
Plato, in the Timæus, that it would be a vain

attempt to unfold the sublimest truths to the Vulgar, as the eyes of the multitude were not strong enough to look at truth.

As with the ancient religions and schools of philosophy, so a conviction of this kind perplexed all along the teaching of Christ and St. Paul. God Himself, and the divine authority of His laws as written in the soul of man from the foundation of the world, were obliged to be impersonated, symbolized, and transfigured in every possible form, in order to be understood by the practical, hard-minded Jews and their Gentile contemporaries. Christ impersonated, as the Son of God, his own divine spirit—his own intensity of heavenly sentiment, in order to bring his ideas into communication with those he addressed. All that he saw in nature, he converted into metaphorical allusions to the mystic spirit of Truth and Love burning ever brightly within his soul.

XXV.

FAITH AND REASON HAVE SEPARATE PROVINCES AND MODES OF PERCEPTION.

Our Reason and Intellect are limited;—although their range of action extends from the astral spaces of the Universe to the smallest atoms of the micro-

scopic world, and over the whole moral interior of
man, still there are boundaries which they cannot
transcend. They must stop on arriving at First
Causation. Trained Inductive Intellect can go no
further. It is then that Faith begins. Man, being
finite, cannot grasp the Infinite; but just as all
the phenomena of the objective and human worlds
come legitimately within the province of the mental
faculties, so does the Unknown, the Invisible, and
the Mystic, come within the sphere of the Psychical.
Hence Faith, and Religious belief. The Known
world we apprehend by demonstration; the Unknown by Faith, or Psychical intuition. Whatever
is objective cannot belong to Faith, which is essen-
tially subjective. What error, therefore, to present
evidence of an objective nature to the appreciation
of Faith! Metaphysicians and men of science,
indeed, erect imperfect systems, in which Faith is
ignored; and theological writers, on their side,
justly offend the common sense of the intellectual
classes by taking visible phenomena out of the
domain of philosophic inquiry, and hedging them
round with miraculous interpretation. On the
other hand, Spinosa, without Faith, and transforming his Reason into Perceptive intellect, conceived
the pantheistic idea of seeing God, or modifications
of God, in all the parts of the Universe, bringing

his system to a level with the Pagan mythologies, but without their impersonations. Infidelity and Superstition are equally removed from Truth.

XXVI.

INTELLECTUAL INTERPRETATION OF THE BIBLE NECESSARY.

The same rules of enlightened criticism ought now to be reverently directed to the traditional Theology of our times, as have been already applied with such skill and success to the Mosaic Geology. A new and more intellectual interpretation of biblical truths will be the result. The symbols, impersonations, and deifications of our Christian mythology will then be presented, more as expressions of the Psychical forces within Humanity, than as Objective realities having substance and forms of being of their own.

XXVII.

CHRIST DISCOVERED THE TRUTHS OF CHRISTIANITY IN THE INTERIOR OF HIS OWN SOUL.

Our knowledge of the Future, and of our destiny, can only be revealed from an analysis of our Psychical nature. The law of our Being, as indicating the end and aim of our creation, can only be ascertained from the structure and functions of our soul and intellectual system. All revelation has come from this source alone. It is God *within* who has spoken, and not God without. The Subjective has been mistaken for the Objective. Hence every so-called divine manifestation, since the great miracle of the Creation, comes naturally within the pale and liberty of Humanity, without exception whatever — all, visions, prophecies, revelations, miracles. And what need that we should think otherwise?

Like the great Hebrew Prophets of the Old Testament, it was by turning inwards on himself, and feeling the inspiration of sublime Faith, that Christ discovered the momentous truth of the Atonement — the supreme law and transforming element of the moral world, and our sole warrant for the means of the continuous development of the human race. Guided by the Light of his own exalted nature, and looking further than mortal ever did before into the inner truths and mysteries which God Himself, at the beginning, had written in the human soul, to be unfolded in the fulness of time, He revealed the ways of God to man, and that body of divine doctrines, which must ever preside over the remedial agencies for sin, sorrow, and aberration, as well as over the moral and religious improvement of man ; viz., Faith in our

Atoning Conscience in the sight of God within us,
Hope of Another Life, and Charity towards all
mankind.

From constant meditation on these Psychical
truths, in solitude and seclusion from the haunts
of men, He became at last, as it were, That which
he thought and felt. The man Christ became the
Christ Psychical. The mortal lapsed into the
immortal. The spiritual transcended the corporeal
powers of his nature, so that from the time He
resolved to announce the glad tidings of his discovery to his fellow-men, he knew well the fate
which awaited him, and that, from the necessity of
his position, His great mission and His life were
pledged together. With this sorrowful foreboding,
he journeyed to Jerusalem, and apostrophized the
guilty city with that outburst of soul so finely
described in the Bible, his frame no doubt at-
tenuated by a life-long communion with God, and
his eye bright with the fire of prophecy. The final
struggle of his soul in the garden of Gethsemane,
and His godlike words and deportment to the
end, are unapproachable for sublimity and pathos.
Man, though he was, like ourselves, who could
refuse the homage of his love and adoration to so
perfect a being? And who can wonder at the
Divine power, which he evoked out of the depths
of the human soul, becoming indivinized in his

Person by the Mysticism and enthusiastic piety of the early Christians? " The bread of life is he " which cometh down from heaven, and giveth " life unto the world."

XXVIII.

PSYCHICAL DEVELOPMENT NECESSARY AS THE SPIRITUAL GERM OF ANOTHER LIFE.

Man is a finite being, existing by the will of God, with limited faculties, and with a limited known intellectual horizon, beyond which is the Infinite and the Unknown. We are certain, therefore, there exist ranges and forms of Being, which transcend the sphere of Humanity. Besides the Known there exists the Unknown, for which we have a warrant not only in the deductions of Reason, but in a special provision to that effect in the constitution of the Soul. God Himself has deposited there this mystic intimation of " Another World," to guide our footsteps across the threshold of mortality, and to scale the Empyrean. It is evidenced in the creeds and pious rites of Sepulture amongst the races of men, and confirmed by the divine authority of Plato, of St. Paul, and of Christ. This Faith, or psychical belief, is the voice of God within our subjective interior, revealing to

us the wonderful truth, that a constituent part of
our nature will survive the destruction of the
mortal body, with which it has been transitorily
conjoined, and unfold powers of spiritual life in
another state of existence under new conditions
and new modes of Being, but which, as finite
creatures, we have not present faculties to apprehend now. It is the new heavens, the new earth,
and the new Jerusalem of the Apocalypse—"a
" building of God, an house not made with hands,
" eternal in the heavens." "Eye hath not seen, nor
" ear heard, neither have entered into the heart of
" man the things, which God hath prepared for
" them that love him."

For this continuation of individual identity into
another state of existence, for this fusion with
God, a sufficient degree of Psychical development
is absolutely necessary. This portion of Divinity
within us, being of the substance of the world to
come, is the connecting link between God and
Man—the Creator and the creature. It makes
" the last Adam a quickening spirit, the Lord from
" heaven." According to the Evangelical formula,
it is the treasure laid up in heaven—belief in
Christ, the Concrete expression of the Abstract
psychical ideas.

As there must be a basis to constitute every
system of life, spiritual as well as organic, so this

Psychical element failing from want of development, it necessarily follows, the defective individual would be in danger of perishing, with respect to his spiritual nature, in those cases where there are no sufficient conditions of vitality and continuance. In the emphatic words of Christ he must perish everlastingly. And this is only in accordance with the general laws presiding over the other kingdoms of organic life in the great Creation; where arrest of development leads to the destruction of defective individuals, whether in plants or animals. In these conclusions, therefore, both Divinity and Philosophy perfectly agree.

XXIX.

PROGRESSIVE ENHANCEMENT OF RELIGIOUS SYSTEMS.

As in geology we see there are successive systems of creation, one rising above the other, so in mythology and religion, has there been a succession of systems, one transcending the other, beginning with idolatry in India and Egypt, through Greece and Rome; through the unity of structure pervading the Jewish theocracy and Platonism, down to the last link of modern Christianity; from the symbolization of simple perception and passion, down to the mystic impersonations of the present day.

" So on our heels a fresh perfection treads,
" A power more strong in beauty, born of us
" And fated to excel us, as we pass
" In glory, that old Darkness :— nor are we
" Thereby more conquered than by us the rule
" Of shapeless Chaos."   *Hyperion.*

XXX.

DISCOVERY OF PHYSICAL AND PSYCHICAL LAWS ANALOGOUS.

What the Philosophers are to intellectual knowledge; the Prophets, the Evangelists, the Messiahs and Divines are to Faith and psychical truths.   Newton discovered in the Infinity of space the great universal law of gravitation; as Christ discovered in the interior of the Soul the supreme law of the Atonement.

XXXI.

Philosophers are governed by Reason; the pious and evangelical by Faith; the great mass of mankind by Authority, Tradition, and Dogma.

XXXII.

The Past, the Present, the Future, Foreknowledge, Predestination, Fate, are terms only applicable to finite minds — not to God.

XXXIII.

THE HOLY GHOST AND MIRACLES, CONCRETE EXPRESSIONS OF DIVINE AGENCY, THE ONE INTERNAL, THE OTHER EXTERNAL.

Just as the *Numen,* or actual presence of the Deity, was recognized in ancient times, so the Holy Ghost resolves itself into being the concrete equivalent of our Faith in subjective divine agency within the Soul, the germ of which has been deposited in the constitution of our Psychical nature by God himself. Being an innate faculty, it is in this sense independent of the visible world, and an ultimate psychical truth for the recognition of our intellectual powers. By its internal activity, through prayer, we have direct communion with God. It is the foundation of the mystic life within us, and the exclusive source of revelations, religious visions, and prophecies. When Objective Perception, Faith, and Wonder act together, belief in miracles is the result. In that case the idea of Providential agency, which is Faith with Reason, is seen in the Concrete. Belief in miracles is thus the Concrete expression of the idea of Providence in the Abstract.

XXXIV.

A portion of divinity must form an integral part of human nature, to enable us to approach God in our ideas of the Universe and of the Soul. Without this we could not put ourselves in relation to Him, and adore with reverence and intelligence the mystic infinity of his Almighty Being.

XXXV.

CHRIST CRUCIFIED, THE EXTERNAL SYMBOL OF OUR ATONING CONSCIENCE.

" Christ crucified" is for us an external symbol of spiritual Atonement—an ideal sin-offering without bounds or measure for the sins of the whole world, a representation qualified to satisfy our idea of the eternal justice of God. What the vicarious sacrifice of the Scape-Goat was on a small scale, in the Jewish Atonement, for the sins of a single people, that of Christ, the Lamb of God, the theological incarnation of all that is holy and divine, is in the Christian Atonement, for the sins of all mankind. This general idea of satisfaction to eternal justice lays the foundation in the Christian mind for the spiritual theory of the Redemption and Salvation of the world. It is the understood means of grace in order to attain the position of being purified or justified of sin, by belief and repentance, effecting thereby an elevation to Truth and God, and constituting the spiritual germ in the so-called sons of God, which is to expand and fulfil its destiny in another state of Being.

In other words, Conscience holds its sessions in the soul, with God as judge, that sin may be punished by repentance and remorse, that atonement and self-sacrifice may follow, and that spiritual regeneration and redemption may prepare the penitent so-called Son of God for the life to come. Thus Conscience, armed with divine will, becomes justice in action, foreshadowing judgment and punishment. Hence the necessity of Atonement by self-sacrifice, and Christ is born in our souls—the supreme distinctive feature of Christian psychology.

XXXVI.

INTELLECTUAL INTERPRETATION OF THE ATONEMENT.

The development of the idea of an Atoning Conscience, as a divine appointment of our nature, represented objectively by the Passion of Christ, will be the next great step in the advance of Christianity. The application of the outward symbol of Christ crucified to this inner, spiritual and more personal agency within the soul, becomes now a logical necessity to satisfy the more advanced intellectual demands of the age. When attained, it will bring within the pale of Christianity and of the Church, the intellectual classes of society, hitherto virtually excluded by mistaken and unreasonable definitions of Faith, and by the impossible dogmas and traditions of the infant Christian world, still reigning supreme as Orthodox opinion. We must emerge out of this infant period of figure and Impersonation and the dramatized action of Divine Power, by eating, as perfect men, the strong meat of Faith and Reason, and seeing Truth face to face. The necessity for thus penetrating by direct means into the Psychical interior of man, will no doubt ensue in proportion as society advances in knowledge of causation and abstract ideas, as applied to acknowledge the

authority of innate Christian Faith, and rightly
to interpret the *prima philosophia* of the oracles
of God, constituting that faith. These are the
spiritual forces which sweep across the chords of
the soul, and never fail to assert their mystic
predominance over the thoughts and imagination
of man, as soon as the age of worldly ambition has
passed away, and the individual feels conscious he
is approaching the latter end of the procession of
life.

XXXVII.

The physical sciences are a modern creation
from the discoveries of the last half-century; whilst
our theology and religious form of belief date back
fifteen centuries ago. It is time some further
progress should now be made.

XXXVIII.

A SUMMARY OF CHRISTIAN TRUTHS AS TAUGHT BEFORE CHRIST.

By Moses, the Unity of God from Faith, and
the idea of First Causation, subjectively and
objectively.

By Pythagoras, a Judging Conscience on the acts and thoughts of men.

By Anaxagoras, the Unity of the Deity from the idea of First Causation, objectively.

By Socrates, an innate sense of Right and Wrong. — The moral government of the world.

By Plato, the Spirituality and Immortality of the Soul.

By Christ, a Judging and Atoning Conscience in the sight of God within us, Hope in Another Life, and Charity to all mankind.

XXXIX.

THE PSYCHICAL SYSTEM, A CONSTITUENT PART OF HUMAN NATURE.

When we examine within the limit of our powers, the archetypal idea which was in the mind of God when He made man, we shall find that not only did He endow him with reason and a perfect intellectual system, to comprehend the Universe, and Himself as the First Cause, but that He impressed His image upon the soul in order to illuminate and guide him with divine knowledge in the accomplishment of his spiritual destiny. From this source we derive our Faith,

E

Revelation, and mystic communion with God. Conjoined with Causality, it constitutes Truth and Divine Reason, the λογος; divested of external symbols and impersonations, it constitutes the esoteric essence of Christianity—the Christ within us; the Judging and Atoning Conscience in the sight of God; Love of humanity; and Hope of immortal life through the efficient development of our spiritual nature.

Broken, inchoate rudiments of this innate psychical system can be traced even in the idol-worship of the low-typed, perishable races of men, and in the dedicative meaning of the colossal temples and religious monuments of Egypt, India, Mexico, and the classical antique world.

XL.

MAN WAS CREATED IN DIVERSITY OF TYPE TO BE FINALLY DEVELOPED IN TIME BY GOD'S LAW INTO UNITY.

There certainly was a time when man did not exist on the earth. The Almighty Word went forth, and the different races of men, most probably in all the integrity of adult age, peopled the continents and islands of the globe. As we can hardly conceive, and much less know, the mode and proximate causes of this creation, it is only philosophical to attribute at once the origin of man to First Causation, or the will of God. Neither natural selection, nor the blind chance of external agency, can ever account for that intelligent unity of design which we see pervading each and every typical system of organic life. The accommodating plasticity of nature must ever hold a subordinate relation to these pre-existing typical forms, whose origin is lost in First Causation. The theories of Lamarck, Darwin, and of " the Vestiges," might well explain modifications of organic development within very limited ranges, but they are as far from truth in one extreme as the worst cases of abject superstition in the other. There is a law, a purpose, and an end in the human system, commensurate with the dignity and grandeur of an Almighty conception.

Many philosophical writers have shown that since the historical ages the different varieties of man have been undergoing the operation of a law bringing them into one type, or character, and that this is the characteristic result of every movement towards civilization. All the Diversities of race melt into Unity.

But it is the general opinion at present, in all Christian nations, that the creation of man was confined to a single pair, Adam and Eve, and that he subsequently degenerated from the perfection of his original nature, an opinion embodying the dogmas of the Fall of Man, and Original Sin, as handed down to us by Jewish tradition, made sacred by the authority and adoption of Orthodox Churches, and supported by an incredible amount of erudition and scientific research, which however loses its value from being the special pleading of foregone conclusions.

Are we right, therefore, in adhering to the Mosaic tradition of our descent from One pair, when it proves to be in direct contradiction to the great law of Humanitary progress, which has prevailed since the historical times, viz. the tendency and fusion of all the races of the earth towards Unity, as an ultimate end, both of physical type and civilization? If the law of progress is bringing mankind from Diversity to Unity, how could this diversity of races have sprung from One pair alone? How can Diversity proceed from Unity, when the laws of progress are producing Unity from Diversity?

The original pair, according to the Mosaic tradition, was created in perfection, and the defects and imperfections of man were after consequences. But admitting man was created in diversity and original imperfection, the different races of the world would constitute the raw material and rudimental elements of human nature, but containing within its sealed-up systems, adequate latent capabilities which would collectively carry the race to its highest perfection, when in the fulness of time these capabilities had become developed by the laws of progress and civilization. Every race, every generation, every individual, would thus have a duty and an object in concurring according to their powers and opportunities to further this appointed mission of man on earth, by their labour, their intelligence, and their moral will—a grand work of God with Whom the whole family of man would be fellow-labourers.

So that, independently of adverse and fatal physiological reasons to our origin from One pair, it will be one day acknowledged, that the creation of the species took place universally during primeval epochs of formative activity, from the lowest Australian type to the highest Caucasian, representing Man in every variety of race; that he was launched upon the theatre of his existence in an undeveloped state, with numerous diversities of type, the great law and end of his nature being the progressive evolution of latent powers; and that in his march towards ideal civilization and perfection, the different races of the earth are destined to concur and contribute their part, collectively and individually, until the Great Unity, intended by God, should be effected; or to speak biblically, the divine Covenant of the creation be fulfilled.

In this appointed course of Humanity, the weak, unfitted, or intractable elements will disappear, as, under the contact and supremacy of the superior races, the lower-typed savage populations melt away beyond recall with the certainty of a natural law.

Thus an unceasing movement towards fusion and Unity is the great law of Humanity, presiding over the life and development of nations and individuals, under whose operation the original diversity and plurality of races will ultimately disappear. It is the supreme law of God upon earth, whose consummation was typically prefigured in past religious ages, through the prophetic light of psychical inspiration, by the Millennium, the Second Coming of Christ, and the universal prevalence of Christianity.

London : — STRANGEWAYS & WALDEN (late G. BARCLAY), Printers,
Castle St. Leicester Sq.